PRESQUE ISLE
State Park

A Scenic Tour of the Peninsula

Majestic Remembrance...
Perry Monument

Kevin-John Jobczynski

Publisher....... *Matthew D. Walker Publishing*
Design Director....... *Matthew Walker*
Designers....... *Anthony Orlando, Matthew Walker*
Photo Editors....... *Art Becker, Matthew Walker*
Design Consultant.......*Shelle Barron*
Additional Writers.......*Evelyn Anderson, Randy Neyer*
Readers....*Toby Cunningham, Jean Stull, Aimee Nicolia, Gloria Walker,*
                Bob Walker, Don Guerrein, Paula Guerrein
Printed in The United States of America
Pre-Press.......*Digital Alchemy*

© 2000 Matthew D. Walker Publishing
111 Columbia Circle
Erie, Pa 16505
All Rights Reserved
Published 2000

First Edition
ISBN Number: 0-9704875-0-9

PRESQUE ISLE
State Park

Matthew Walker

Wilda Sundberg

Foreword

Some names can instantly take you back to your childhood. Like Presque Isle State Park. I have been coming to Presque Isle since I was old enough to stand - walking its beaches, biking its trails, or just watching the birds and other wildlife play on a lazy afternoon. If I close my eyes I can recall the sights and sounds and smells of this extraordinary place, and it never fails to put a smile on my face.

But why rely on memories when you can have the real thing? Recently I found myself fishing on the Lake - and catching a beautiful sunrise. On another occasion I walked along the beach to catch an equally beautiful sunset. It's a special place that can draw you in like that. And this natural wonderland is certainly special to me. I hope you enjoy this book as much - and as often - as I enjoy Presque Isle State Park itself.

- Governor Tom Ridge

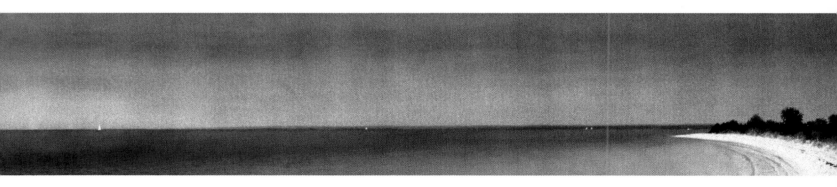

Lee Steadman

What is Presque Isle?

*A*long the lakeshore of northwestern Pennsylvania, there is a long, thin peninsula which juts into Lake Erie. When French explorers saw this peninsula they named it **Presque Isle** which means "almost an island". This is a very special place, and this book captures some of its beauty.

The natural environment of Presque Isle is unique. It is one of the only spots in the world where you can observe plant succession from seedlings on the shoreline to a climax stage forest within a short walk. It is also one of the best birding sites in North America. Because of these attributes, Presque Isle became a National Natural Landmark in 1969.

In the summer, Presque Isle is packed with folks who come to boat, to fish, or to enjoy a day at the peninsula's seven miles of beaches. At nightfall, you can watch one of the most beautiful sunsets in the world. In winter, Presque Isle is a great place for cross-country skiing, ice fishing, or hiking. Presque Isle is a treasure for Pennsylvania and a gift for anyone who chooses to discover it.

Photos by Don Dombrowski, Lucia Surmik O.S.B., Bob Grubbs, John Horstman, and Art Becker

Sam Stull

Chapter One
Natural Environment

13 Introduction
15 Geographic Location
16 Formation
17 Erosion
18 Succession
19 Ponds and Lagoons
20 Sands and Soil
21 Dunes
22 Weather Effects
24 Sunsets

Chapter Two
Plants & Wildlife

29 Introduction
30 From the Park Naturalist
31 Reptiles / Amphibians
33 Mammals
34 Trees
36 Wildflowers
38 Grass and Mushrooms
39 Insects
40 Birds
43 Gull Point

Chapter Three
History

45 Introduction
46 Time Table
48 Joe Root
49 Eriez Indian Skeleton
50 Flagship Niagara
52 Battle of Lake Erie
53 Rebuilding The Niagara
54 USS Wolverine
54 Cranberry Day
55 Alien Encounter
56 Road System
57 State Park History/Officials
58 Lifeguards

Chapter Four
Recreation

61 Introduction
62 Beaches
65 Sunset Point / Kite Beach
67 Winter Recreation
69 Hiking Trails
70 Multi-Purpose Trail
71 Fishing
73 Boating
74 Marina / Channel
75 Swimming

Chapter Five
Structures

77 Introduction
78 Peninsula Businesses
80 The Feather
81 Stull Interpretive Center
82 Waterworks
83 Houseboats
84 Presque Isle Lighthouse
88 Shelters / Admin. Building
89 Perry Monument
90 North Pier Light
91 Coast Guard Station

End Pages

Profile of Artists 92
Artists Associations 95
Maps 96-101
Images 102 - 107
Bibliography 108
Presque Isle Partnership 109
Contacts 109
Artists 110
Acknowledgments & Thanks 111

Jack Paluh

The Birth of Presque Isle...an Eriez Indian Legend

After Manitou, the Great Spirit, had created the world with its mountains and its valleys, with its forests full of game and its lakes and streams full of fish, he led his favorite children, the Eriez Indians, to the shores of the great unsalted sea and spoke to them thus:

"This is the place, my children, which your father the Great Spirit has chosen for the site of your villages. The hills and the plains abound in game to feed and clothe you. The pure water from streams will slake your thirst. The fields will yield a hundred fold returns from the labors of your women. The lake will furnish you fish in abundance. The sun rising beyond the mountains in the east will give you life and the cool breezes coming from the land of snow and ice will strengthen your sons and daughters in mind and body, so that you, my favorite children, may be the pride of your race."

The Eriez, obedient to the wishes and commands of Manitou, lived on the shores of the lake. They hunted the buffalo and the deer on the plains and the panther and the bear in the mountains. The women tilled the fields which yielded maize and pumpkins in abundance. The fishermen in their birch-bark canoes rode the waters of the lake and their labor was bountifully repaid, for the blessing of the Great Spirit was with them. Their canoes returned to the shores heavily laden with fish from the depths of the water.

One day the fishermen paddled their canoes far out into the lake to find the place where the sun sank into the waters. The spirits of the lake were angered at the boldness of the fishermen and caused a storm to rise. Whipped by the fury of the wind, large waves rocked the fishermen's frail canoes before them.

When the darkness of the night came, the flashes of lightning showed the fishermen fighting for their lives and appealing to the Great Spirit for help in this, their hour of peril. The Great Spirit was moved to pity by the cries of distress from his favorite children. To protect his favorite children, Manitou stretched out his left arm and placed it in the raging waters shielding the fishermen from the fury of the storm. Behind his sheltering arm, the fishermen rowed their canoes in safety to the shore.

When the great Spirit lifted his arm from the water, a peninsula shaped like an arm was formed. For all ages, this peninsula will act as a shelter and harbor of refuge for his favorite children, the Eriez.

- author unknown

Art Becker

Geographic Location

Formation

Erosion

Succession

Ponds and Lagoons

Sands and Soils

Dunes

Weather Effects

Sunsets

Natural Environment

Historically, Presque Isle has been estimated to be about 3,200 acres. However, recent studies show that it is closer to half that size. In reality, changing water levels and erosion keep the size and shape of Presque Isle in a constant state of change.

Sam Stull

Geographic Location

Presque Isle is located in the northeastern United States in the Commonwealth of Pennsylvania.

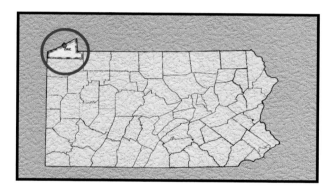

Presque Isle extends from the northwestern corner of Pennsylvania.

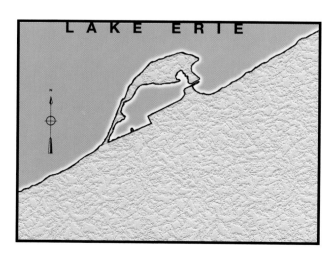

The peninsula is a portion of the southern shoreline that juts out into Lake Erie.

Presque Isle can be reached by PA Rte 832 (Peninsula Drive) which is accessible from U.S. Rte 20 and U.S. Rte 5 and I-90.

Sam Stull

How Presque Isle was Formed

Geologists believe that at the end of the last ice age (11,000 years ago) a large slow moving glacier pushed a moraine southward into the valley which is now filled with Lake Erie. This moraine, which is made up of clay, sand, and gravel, is just 30-50 feet below the surface of the lake.

In the years since that ice age, the waters of Lake Erie have carved away huge pieces of land along the coast of Pennsylvania forming bluffs 60 feet high or more. The sediment which has eroded into Lake Erie, has been sorted out by waves. Sand and pebbles have been deposited along the shoreline to form a beach. Lake Erie storms and high energy westerly winds have taken some of this sediment and moved it along the coast. Some of this debris eventually got caught up on the moraine and formed the peninsula.

The shape and size of Presque Isle has changed dramatically as it has moved along the moraine. In fact, it has been estimated by renowned botanist Dr. O.E. Jennings, that Presque Isle has been migrating eastward at the rate of one-half mile per century. At its current position the tip of Presque Isle (Gull Point) is at the eastern edge of the moraine.

Erosion

Lake Erie storms and prevailing westerly winds keep the shape of Presque Isle in a constant state of change. Waves wash up on the peninsula in a diagonal direction and move sand and pebbles to the east. Sand may travel along the entire length of Presque Isle in just a few days. Most of the sand is then carried back into the lake while some of it moves around the peninsula forming sand bars.

Erosion and Lake Erie storms have broken through the neck of the peninsula at least four times since 1819. As part of the plan to keep the peninsula connected to the shore, massive quantities of sand have been deposited at the neck of Presque Isle. The combination of this beach replenishment and a series of stone breakwalls which have been constructed to soften wave action have kept Presque Isle attached to the mainland, but not without their price. The breakwalls have resulted in a saw-tooth shaped beach. Along with a change in the shoreline's aesthetics, this method has had other effects on the ecological balance of the peninsula.

John Fontecchio

John Buffington

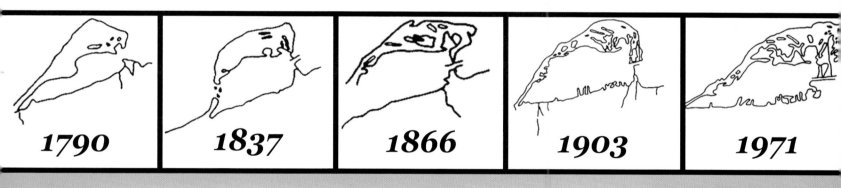

1790   **1837**   **1866**   **1903**   **1971**

Erie County Historical Society and Museum

Charles Ventrello

The photograph above shows the neck of the peninsula washed away separating it from the mainland. Presque Isle has become an island many times throughout its history. In efforts to control nature, various methods including bulkhead, groin, and jetties have been tried. The most recent attempt to slow down Mother Nature has been the breakwalls.

Bob Hagle

Mary Hamilton

Succession

One feature which makes Presque Isle unique is its biological progression. Within a short walk on the peninsula, you can observe 600 years of plant succession. Presque Isle is among a handful of places in the world where this occurs.

The 6 distinct ecological zones on Presque Isle include:
1. Lake Erie, Presque Isle Bay, and the shoreline
2. Sand plain and new ponds
3. Dunes and ridges
4. Old ponds and marshes
5. Thicket and sub-climax forest
6. Climax forest

Bob Hagle

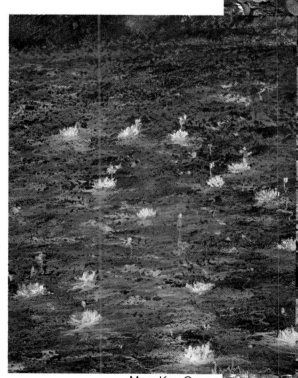
Mary Kay Geary

Sam Stull

Ponds and Lagoons

The interior of Presque Isle is made up of a series of ponds. Some of these ponds were connected in the 1930s for the purpose of recreation. This group of ponds is commonly referred to as the lagoons. The area is ideal for fishing and canoeing.

A spider plays Hide and Seek in the sand at Presque Isle.

Sands and Soils

A major reason for the peninsula's diverse biological progression is the variety of soils. Lakefront sand supports grasses and shrubs while inland soils with more organic material can support a mature ecosystem. Along the lakefront, sand has eroded resulting in a "shifting" peninsula. In efforts to replace some of the sand which has eroded, sand has been both dredged from the lake and trucked onto Presque Isle from other areas and dumped onto the neck of the peninsula.

Evelyn Askey Zaleski

Denise Keim

Dunes

During the winter months, ice dunes can be seen along the peninsula's shoreline. The dunes are built up by a combination of lake ice, wave surge, and freezing spray.

Sand ridges can be seen at the tip of Presque Isle *(see page 19)*. The ridges help geologists track the growth and erosion of the peninsula.

Judy Emling

Weather Effects

Lake Erie is by far the shallowest of the Great Lakes. Because the lake is so shallow, violent storms can build up quickly and hit hard, particularly in the spring and fall. Westerly winds can travel over a great distance on Lake Erie before landing on the peninsula and the mainland. While the forces of wind and wave action can be destructive, they are also elements which initially helped create Presque Isle.

Lake Erie also has the widest seasonal fluctuations in water temperature of the Great Lakes. Air masses which effect the peninsula are **Maritime Tropical** *(warm and moist air which flow north from the Gulf of Mexico)*, **Continental Polar** *(cooler, drier air traveling south from Canada)*, and **Maritime Polar** *(which originates over the north Pacific Ocean)*.

Because Presque Isle is geographically located where it is, spring, summer, fall, and winter are all displayed in full force. The natural beauty of the park can be seen throughout the year.

"I can hear my granddad's stories, of the storms out on Lake Erie where vessels, and cargo, and fortunes, and sailors' lives were lost."

- James Taylor
Millworker

courtesy of Presque Isle State Park

Maybe your dad wasn't lying when he said that it snowed more when he was younger. A car takes a leisurly drive down a well plowed Peninsula Drive.

Jim McEnery

Lake Erie waves pound the shoreline.

Lee Steadman

Charles Ventrello

Eric LaPrice

top: *Presque Isle Bay freezes over frequently.*

bottom right: *A water spout can be seen forming over Lake Erie.*

bottom left: *Severe ice storms can be both beautiful and destuctive.*

Sunsets

John Horstman

Art Becker

It's true that Presque Isle has some of the most beautiful sunsets in the world. Visitors travel from afar to enjoy the breathtaking site.

Eric LaPrice

Roy Ahlgren

Louis A. Colussi

Louis A. Colussi

Bob Hagle

Judy Emling

Don Dombrowski

John Hortsman

Susan Hosford Beck

Bob Hagle

Bob Hagle

Laura Beichner O.S.B.

Lucia Surmik O.S.B.

Lynn Weissert O.S.B.

Margret Ann Pilewski O.S.B.

Ann Muczynski O.S.B.

Bob Grubbs

From the Park Naturalist

Reptiles and Amphibians

Mammals

Trees

Wildflowers

Grass

Mushrooms

Insects

Birds

Plants and Wildlife

From the Park Naturalist

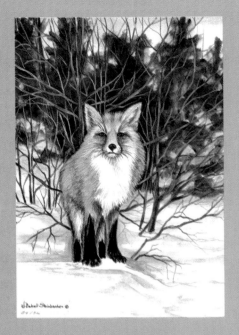

*A*s a *naturalist* I look at the Presque Isle peninsula as a "gift of nature" to admire in all its beauty, diversity and mysteries. An ecosystem of sand, plants and animals, equal to no other system I know, that offers a chance to learn, discover and wonder with every sunrise. Peacefulness meets each sunset as visitors leave and the animal inhabitants come to life.

Both the cultural and natural history continue to provide visitors a chance to look into the past and imagine the future. Nothing compares to the eyes of a child as stories are told and lessons taught of days gone by.

Thankfully, land management practices of current day reflect conservation and preservation. The past was not so kind. Currently there are nearly one hundred plants, animals, and ecosystems of state or federal concern, some that are lost forever. It is important that the child who learns today has the opportunity to teach in the future. Through the eyes of a naturalist this is our future. More...not less.

Randy A. Neyer
Presque Isle State Park Naturalist

paintings by Vi Bebell Steinbacher

Reptiles & Amphibians

Reptiles and Amphibians found on Presque Isle include frogs, toads, turtles, snakes, salamanders, and others.

Sam Stull

Mammals

The peninsula is home to a variety of animals including White-Tailed Deer, Red Foxes, beavers, raccoons, several species of squirrels, Eastern Cottontails, a variety of mice, moles and shrews, eastern chipmunks, coyotes, striped skunks and opossums.

Trees

For such a small area of land, Presque Isle boasts a wide variety of trees including cottonwoods, Black Cherry, Northern Red Oak, Red Maple, Eastern Hemlock, and many more.

Evelyn Anderson

Pines are among the dominant tree species at intermediate stages of succession on dunes and dry sand plains.

Cottonwoods steal the show in this wonderland peninsula that is so aptly named Presque Isle.

It isn't that the cottonwoods are handsome, like the black oaks, or as graceful as the pin oaks growing in the park - for they aren't. Nor do they produce stunning colored leaves in the fall, like those of the tupelos. Their flowers aren't especially attractive, and certainly not fragrant, like those of the northern locust. But, cottonwoods attract attention in their own grand way.

When the cottonwoods release their billions of cottony-tipped seeds, Presque Isle is turned into a delightful land of make-believe, with early June looking like mid-winter as the seeds float through the air, create blizzards, pile up in drifts, catch on the leaves and stems of plants and decorate spider webs.

Each year, after that unforgettable show - a show that has been going on for hundreds of years - something very special begins to happen.

The cottonwood seeds quickly germinate in wet, loose sand around newly formed ponds. The seedlings grow fast, and as their lower branches catch drifting sand, dunes begin to form.

Since those dunes have long been Presque Isle's own natural first line of defense against storms which threaten to wash this amazing sandspit away, it is evident that those rather plain, ordinary looking cottonwoods have helped give us the Presque Isle that is enjoyed by thousands of people every year.

- Evelyn Anderson

Jeff Urraro

Mike Campbell

Dan Byler

Wildflowers

Each year, from late March through early November, there is a continuous pagent of colorful wildflowers throughout the park displaying themselves at beaches, meadows, forests, and wetlands.

Jean Stull

*P*resque Isle is a botanical paradise. There is no other place of similar size in Pennsylvania that has as many of the state's endangered, threatened and rare species as are found here. For more than two hundred years, it has lured botanists.

Each of its many habitats - its sandy beaches, thickets, ponds, lagoons, and climax forest - provides the habitats needed for a vast variety of plants and inter-related species to survive.

On the beaches can be found sea rocket, a plant which sailors used to eat to prevent scurvy. There are thickets of fragrant bayberries that produce an abundance of berries which are food for yellow-rumped warblers and several other species of birds. Along the edges of some of the ponds can be found insect-eating blatterworts; in the ponds is wild rice which provides food for waterfowl; and in the climax forest are Indian pipes which, because they have no chlorophyll, get their food for survival from a fungus living in the soil.

There are a number of unusually beautiful plants at Presque Isle - like the wild lupine, wild roses, obedient plant, fringed gentian, Canada anemone, rose mallow, pickerel-weed, the water lilies and the Indian grass.

Some of the Park's alien plants are also attractive - like the invasive purple loosestrife, Japanese honey-suckle and Oriental bittersweet, which, unfortunately, take over native habitats. Fortunately, there is a constant vigil at Presque Isle to preserve Pennsylvania's valuable assets.

- Evelyn Anderson

Sam Stull

Evelyn Anderson

Grass

Sturdy grass and Golden Rod play a critical role in the stabilization of the sand dunes. Grasses in particular arrive at the early stages of succession and pave the way for the plant species that follow.

Evelyn Anderson

courtesy Presque Isle State Park

Mushrooms

The peninsula is home to over 300 species of fleshy fungi. Mushrooms are one of the most mysterious and best kept biological secrets on the park.

Jean Stull

Bob Grubbs

Judy Emling

Gerald McWilliams

Insects

Over 1200 species of insects are found on Presque Isle. Sand dunes harbor ant lions and ponds harbor beetles, caddisflies, bugs, and many more. Just as for birds, the peninsula acts as a "landfall" for migrating Monarch Butterflies.

The nocturnal Northern Saw-whet Owl is spotted on the peninsula in pine plantings and other heavy cover.

Bob Grubbs

Birds

*P*resque Isle is unique in the fact that it is one of the only places in the world with such a diverse biological progression of plant life in such a limited area *(see pg. 18)*. Each group of plants found on the peninsula attracts its own group of birds.

The peninsula's vegetation combined with its geographical location make the park a perfect resting, nesting, and feeding area for hundreds of species of birds - including 45 species of special concern, 6 of which are state or federally endangered, and 6 of which are threatened. Federally endangered species include the Bald Eagle and the Piping Plover.

For a complete map of prime birding sites on Presque Isle see page 101

Bob Grubbs

Bob Grubbs

With 320 species of birds, Presque Isle is the most popular birding site in Pennsylvania. Enthusiasts from around the world travel to the peninsula.

Sam Stull

Jean Stull

Bob Grubbs

Duck Hunting

Duck and goose hunting have been popular activities historically on Presque Isle and continue to be during regulated fall seasons today. Designated and authorized blinds are available.

Erie County Historical Society and Museum

Gull Point

Presque Isle is an extremely fragile and ever-changing piece of land. Perhaps nowhere on the peninsula is this more true than at Gull Point.

Gull Point is located at the northeastern tip of Presque Isle and takes up 319 acres. The area is so fragile, in fact, that 57 of these acres have been designated as a special management area. The special management area is closed to the public from April 1st through November 30th each year.

The best example of the unique plant succession found on Presque Isle is at Gull Point. Many of the plant species found here are threatened or endangered in Pennsylvania. Every year, shorebirds migrate from as far north as the Arctic Circle to as far south as the tip of South America. In their long journey, Presque Isle acts as a safe resting spot. In the spring, breathtaking waves of hawks and smaller birds pass through. Gull Point is also home to many waterfowl and wading birds.

Bob Grubbs

Bob Hagle

Sam Stull

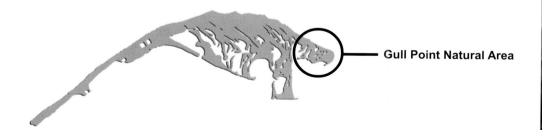

Gull Point Natural Area

Erie County Historical Society and Museum

Time Table

Joe Root

Eriez Indian Skeleton

Flagship Niagara

Battle of Lake Erie

Rebuilding the Niagara

USS Wolverine

Cranberry Day

Alien Encounter

Road System

State Park History & Officials

Lifeguards

History

◄ - 1650
Eriez Indians are the first
known settlers in the region.

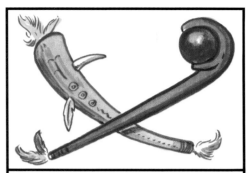

1650
The Iroquois Confederation
defeat the Eriez Indians
in a bloody war.

1720's
French explorers establish
a presence on the peninsula
and name it "Presqu'ile"
which means "almost an island".

1760's
British defeat French in the
Seven Years War
(a.k.a "French and Indian War").

1763
British prevent Indians and French
from trading with each other.
Indians ransack British forts
and burn British settlements.

1776
Colonists fight British and create
The United States of America.

1792
Northwest triangle purchased
by Pennsylvania.

1795
"Mad" Anthony Wayne
overthrows Indians and
the City of Erie is founded.

Bob Lowry

1812-1814
War of 1812. A fleet is built in Erie
which defeats the British in the
Battle of Lake Erie.

1813-1814
Perry's fleet spends a harsh winter
on Presque Isle at Little Bay.
It is renamed Misery Bay.

Bob Grubbs

1857
Pierhead Light (North Pier) built.

Evelyn Askey-Zaleski

1872
Lighthouse built.

1874-1902
Caviar Factory (sturgeon eggs) is in operation at Sturgeon Bay.

Mary Hamilton

1904-1911
Waterworks created.

1921
Presque Isle becomes a State Park.

1924
First paved road on Presque Isle.

John Buffington

1926
Perry Monument built.

1956
Marina Lake created.

1957
Modern Bathhouses built.

Sam Stull

1962-63
Marina, Administration Building and Sewage Plant are all built.

Evelyn Askey-Zaleski

1984
Multi-purpose Bike Trail is constructed on the bay side.

John Buffington

1989-93
Breakwalls are constructed

Bob Grubbs

1994
Presque Isle Partnership is created and Stull Interpretive Center is opened

Bob Lowry

2000
This book is written

illustrations by Mark Weber

Joe Root

Presque Isle's most legendary inhabitant was probably Joe Root.

Raised in Erie, Joe spent his childhood as a fisherman's apprentice devoting most of his time hunting and fishing on the peninsula. Joe also spent some of his youth with the circus where he learned to be a ventriloquist. Eventually, Root made the peninsula his home sleeping in various shanties that he built. Joe Root was famous for expressions such as "ate fried mosquitoes, only the white meat, saved the dark for breakfast." When the kids of the day visited Presque Isle, they loved seeing Joe. He used to watch over them while they were there and he would entertain them with his ventriloquism skills.

Unfortunately, some folks saw Joe Root as a threat. Rumors floated around that he was actually an undercover spy working for a business preparing to acquire the peninsula. Other folks were simply concerned that he might gain squatters rights to the land.

Local authorities put Joe in the County Home several times in the early 1900s but it was hard to keep him there. They eventually would handcuff Root to keep him from drifting back to the peninsula that he loved so much.

Sadly, in 1910 he was committed to the State Hospital for the Insane where he died 2 years later. Some folks say that the sands of Presque Isle are always shifting because they are searching for their beloved Joe Root.

"Ate fried mosquitoes, only the white meat, saved the dark for breakfast."

Erie County Historical Society and Museum

Eriez Indian Skeleton

Jim McEnery

It had been several days into my sister's winter visit in February 1980. We were experiencing a little cabin fever. In spite of the brutally cold temperature outside, it was clear the dogs were ready to go for a walk.

If not for the dogs, we wouldn't have discovered the skeleton stretched out and embedded in the frozen lake bank just east of the peninsula. I had,unsuspectingly, walked over and up to the frozen shoreline to what appeared to be the only semblance of a stick nearby to throw to the dogs. As it turns out, I yanked the poor fellow's femur bone right out of his burial site. A call to a local anthropologist, Jude Kirkpatrick and later the Millcreek Police, determined no foul play. This was the remains of an Eriez Indian who apparently died from an abscessed tooth. Kirkpatrick's crew excavated the entire skeleton as the weather warmed and named it the "McEnery Site." You can see it in a Pittsburgh museum.

- Sue Daley

(Note: My sister left before the thaw and all the excitement of the dig and I wasn't home when Kirkpatrick named this site...my boyfriend was...and when asked, "What's your name anyway?" He answered Jim McEnery. For the record, my sister and I think the site should have been named after US or the dogs...)

Erie County Historical Society and Museum

Flagship Niagara
Building a Fleet at Presque Isle

*I*n 1813, Erie was a small farming community with a population of less than 500. Recognizing the threat of a British invasion, Daniel Dobbins, a Great Lakes shipmaster who lived in Erie, was assigned by the Navy to begin building a fleet.

Dobbins knew that Presque Isle Bay and the peninsula were perfect for the task. There was an abundance of timber and natural resources. There was also a sand bar at the bay's entrance which would prevent the British from easily attacking. Dobbins quickly recruited shipwrights, blockmakers, blacksmiths, caulkers, boat builders and laborers from Pittsburgh, Philadelphia, and elsewhere. The men were paid $2.75 and a pint of whiskey a day to help build the ships. Canvas was brought up from Philadelphia. Iron came from Pittsburgh and Meadville. The cannons came from Washington, D.C. and Saketts Harbor, New York. Dobbins oversaw the project until experienced shipbuilders arrived. Noah Brown, a New York shipbuilder, was recruited to finish the job. A total of 6 vessels were completed including four schooners and two brigs, the Lawrence and the Niagara. The Americans were ready to take on the world's largest navy.

Bob Lowry

The Niagara is distinguished from other sailing ships by its number of masts and rectangular sails.

The Battle of Lake Erie

*O*liver Hazard Perry was born the son of "fighting Quaker parents" in Rhode Island. At age 13, Perry joined the Navy as a midshipman. His career steered him to Africa, Europe, and the Caribbean.

Eventually, Perry was given command of many voyages in the small American Navy. In 1813, he was sent to Erie, Pennsylvania as the relief commander of a fleet preparing to fight the British.

Overcoming great odds, Perry led the fleet to victory at Put-In-Bay, Ohio. He returned to Erie with the great honor of being the first man to defeat an entire British squadron in British history.

The American hero proudly reported to General Harrison, "We have met the enemy and they are ours, two ships, two brigs, one schooner, and one sloop."

John Silk Deckard

"We have met the enemy and they are ours..."

James E. Sabol

In June of 1813, off the coast of Boston, Massachusetts, the U.S.S. Chesapeake was defeated by the British H.M.S. Shannon. The last words of the Chesapeake's dying Captain Lawrence were, "Don't give up the ship."

In Erie, Pennsylvania, later that summer, Commodore Perry took as his flagship the Lawrence. His battle flag read: "Don't Give Up the Ship." Ironically, during the battle, Perry did "give up" the Lawrence, rowed over to the Niagara, hoisted the flag and won the battle. The legendary flag is displayed at the United States Naval Academy.

DONT GIVE UP THE SHIP

Erie County Historical Society and Museum

Rebuilding the Niagara

In the seven years following the Battle of Lake Erie, the Niagara was used as a station ship. In 1820, the ship was moved back over to Misery Bay and sunk for preservation. She stayed submerged there for nearly 100 years.

To celebrate the battle's centennial, in 1913, the hulk was raised out of Misery Bay by the citizens of Erie. Workmen used many of the original boards to rebuild the ship. After she was completed, the Niagara was towed to Put-in-Bay, Ohio, the actual site of the Battle of Lake Erie, for ceremonies. The Flagship was returned to the shores of Presque Isle for her home. Erieites of the day would frequently row across the bay to picnic on the peninsula and visit the ship.

By 1931 the ship had suffered severe decay. The state took on the task of rebuilding her again but the Great Depression stalled the effort. The hull was not completed until 1943 and the mast and rigging were not placed until 1963.

The Niagara was once again in need of serious repair by the early 1980s. A new ship was designed and built by The International Historic Watercraft Society. There are some original timbers which have been used in non-structural places.

Celebrating the 175th anniversary of the Battle of Lake Erie, The Niagara was launched September 10, 1988.

Erie County Historical Society and Museum

Bob Lowry

Bob Lowry

After the American victory in the Battle of Lake Erie, the British threatened revenge. Perry and his men remained in Misery Bay and Erie Harbor during the winter of 1813-1814. Legend has it that throughout that harsh winter many men died of smallpox. Their bodies were buried in a nearby pond which they named Graveyard Pond.

USS Wolverine

Misery Bay was the final resting place for the USS Wolverine, the oldest iron-clad ship in the country. The vessel which was originally named the USS Michigan, was launched in 1843 and had a long career protecting American interests on the Great Lakes. The ship which acted as a Union Navy recruiting station during the Civil War, was decommissioned in 1912 and renamed the USS Wolverine. In the 1900s, the vessel had a long history of political "red tape" regarding ownership and responsibility for restoration and was unfortunately scrapped in 1949.

S.S. WOLVERINE and PERRY MEMORIAL

courtesy of Edna Huntington

David Tousey

Cranberry Day

A popular activity in the 1800s was rowing over to the peninsula to pick cranberries. In fact, the berries, which grew primarily at Cranberry Marsh (now Cranberry Pond) were in such demand that state law made it illegal to pick cranberries before the first Tuesday in October. Thus, was born "Cranberry Day" - the first Tuesday in October.

Erie County Historical Society and Museum

Beach #6 enjoying a summer day that was out of this world.

An Eerie Encounter on Beach 6

An eerie encounter took place at Presque Isle in the summer of 1966. After spending a lazy day at Beach 6, Betty Clem and her friends began to pack up and get ready to head home. When they got back to their car they found it stuck in the sand. After unsuccessfully trying to free the car, two of Betty's friends, Gerald Lobell and DouglasTibetts, went for help. Betty and three other girls waited in the car. When the boys returned with the police, they found the girls screaming hysterically.

According to the girls, they saw a bright light dart across the sky and land about 300 yards away from them on the beach. They silently huddled together in the car in fear. A moment later, the light came toward the car and landed directly on the roof jolting and vibrating the car. Then the girls heard something scratching on the steel roof. Betty peered out the window and found a large gorilla-shaped creature about six feet tall staring back at her. By the time help arrived, the creature was gone.

Beach 6

True facts: A total of 8 sightings were reported in Erie, Pa that night of a large saucer shaped light hovering over the peninsula. Unusual footprints and an unidentified clear liquid were found at the scene. Later, a U.S. Air Force investigation of the event turned up "inconclusive". The women stick to their story. Dan Dascani, Chief of Police said, "I am convinced that the young people at Presque Isle saw something."

Roads

The first keeper of Presque Isle Lighthouse referred to the peninsula as "the loneliest place on earth", most likely because there were no roads.

After becoming a State Park in 1921, Presque Isle was in need of a road which would make the peninsula accessible from Lake Road (now West Lake Road), so Peninsula Drive was constructed in the early 1920s. It ran from Lake Road to just west of Waterworks Park. Originally, the road ran along the beach on the lake side, but after years of contending with Lake Erie storms, in 1948 the Park and Harbor commission rebuilt the road further back from the lake.

With the growing popularity of Presque Isle State Park, by the late 1950s, traffic congestion and parking on the peninsula became a real problem. Construction of a modern 2 lane road has kept traffic running smoothly around the park.

For a complete map of roads on Presque Isle see page 97

The lakeside road originally ran along the beach. After years of Lake Erie storm damage, it was moved further back from the water's edge.

images courtesy of Edna Huntington

State Park History and Officials

*T*he ownership and uses of the peninsula have changed many times throughout the last several hundred years *(see timeline pages 46-47)*.

In the 1800s, ownership of Presque Isle passed from the federal government to the Commonwealth of Pennsylvania, to the City of Erie, then to the Marine Hospital Corporation. By 1871, legislation gave the United States ultimate control of Presque Isle for the purpose of national defense, but Pennsylvania maintained jurisdiction over criminal and civil matters.

In order to create a state park, in 1921, Pennsylvania acquired control of the vast majority of Presque Isle from the federal government. Land surrounding the lighthouse and Coast Guard station remained under federal control. From 1921 to 1971 the Pennsylvania State Park and Harbor Commission operated the park. By 1971 control went to the newly established Department of Environmental Resources. In 1995 the D.E.R. was abolished and the Department of Conservation and Natural Resources (DCNR) and Department of Environmental Protection were created. These groups operate the park today. The Presque Isle Partnership *(see page 109)* was founded in 1994 for the purpose of completing special projects which would not fit in the state's budget. The group works primarily in the private sector but with cooperation from the DCNR.

courtesy Presque Isle State Park

Gary Cardot

Top: A Park naturalist shows some children Presque Isle's wonders.

Below: For many, the one hour trip through the lagoons with a naturalist guide is the highlight of a park visit.

PARK MANAGERS

1921-1923	Pa. State Park and Harbor Commission
6/1/23 to 10/1/25	James Albert Wurzbach
10/1/25 to 4/20/35	Capt. William L. Morrison, Superintendent
7/8/27 to 7/1931	Capt. John S. Kane, Assistant Superintendent
4/22/35 to 5/1939	Ambrose J. Mulligan, Superintendent
5/23/39 to 1/1/55	Millard L. Davis, Superintendent
2/7/55 to 9/12/55	Frank J. Horanic, Superintendent
9/12/56 to 1957	E. S. Radcliffe, Interim Park Superintendent
2/14/57 to 1979	Michael E. Wargo, Park Superintendent
1972 to 1973	Greg Schrum, Assistant Park Superintendent
12/73 to 7/86	Dave H. Coryell, Assistant Park Superintendent
9/79 to 8/89	Eugene V. Giza, Park Superintendent
5/80 to 1/89	Doug J. Parker, Assistant Park Superintendent
7/89 to 8/93	Obediah B. Derr, Assistant Park Manager
8/89 to present	Harry J. Leslie, Park Superintendent
5/94 to present	David J. Rutkowski, Assistant Park Manager
5/96 to present	Matthew A. Marcineck, Assistant Park Manager

Erie County Historical Society and Museum

Erie County Historical Society and Museum

Eric LaPrice

Jostens Photography Studio

Lifeguards

Every summer, bathers at Presque Isle are faithfully protected by Pennsylvania Lifeguards. The guards enjoy a proud reputation for being among the best in the country.

Halstan Williams

Beaches

Sunset Point

Multi-Purpose Trail

Winter Recreation

Hiking Trails

Fishing

Boating

Marina

Channel

Swimming

Vitus J. Kaiser

Recreation

Mark Bowen

courtesy of Edna Huntington

Mark Bowen

Eric LaPrice

Mark Bowen

Joyce Skelley Perowicz

Louis A. Colussi

Erie County Historical Society and Museum

Beaches

Along the lakeside, Presque Isle is blessed with seven miles of sandy beaches. This is the only surf swimming available in Pennsylvania. Beaches are open from Memorial Day through Labor Day unless posted otherwise.

For a complete map of beaches on Presque Isle see page 98

Art Becker

Gary Cardot

Gary Cardot

Gary Cardot

Don Dombrowski

Bob Hagle

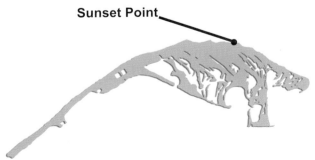

Sunset Point

Sunset Point

Sunset Point is a section of Beach 10 *(see map on page 98)*.
The area is commonly refered to as "Kite Beach" due
to its popularity with kite flyers and wind surfers.

Kate Weber

Presque Isle Bay which freezes over frequently, becomes a popular spot for ice fishing.

Margret Ann Pilewski O.S.B.

Bob Hagle

Louis A. Colussi

Eric LaPrice

Winter Recreation

Presque Isle can be enjoyed throughout the year. During each season, the park offers its own variety of attractions. In the winter months, visitors can enjoy cross-country skiing, iceboating, ice fishing, ice skating, kite skiing, and hiking.

Vitus J. Kaiser

John Horstman

Louis A. Colussi

Eric LaPrice

John Horstman

Eric LaPrice

Eric LaPrice

Hiking Trails

Presque Isle features close to eleven miles of hiking trails. These trails provide a great way to discover some of the interior beauty of the peninsula - much of which is "off the beaten path".

For a complete map of hiking trails
on Presque Isle see page 100

Multi-Purpose Trail

Evelyn Askey

A 10 mile long, paved multi-purpose trail is very popular with in-line skaters, joggers, and cyclists.

Fishing

Both Lake Erie and Presque Isle Bay offer great opportunities for many anglers, while some fishermen prefer to explore the lagoons. Over 100 species of fish are found in Lake Erie.

Bob Hagle

Bob Grubbs

Lee Steadman

HOURS: *The park opens at sunrise and closes at sundown.*

HOTSPOTS: *Lake Erie, Presque Isle Bay, the Lagoons, North Pier*

CATCH: *While fishing Lake Erie, many fishermen go after perch, bass, walleye, salmon, and trout. Presque Isle Bay is abundant in Northern Pike, crappies, perch, bass, and panfish, among others.*

Art Becker

Lee Steadman

Don Dombrowski

Bob Hagle

Bob Grubbs

Bob Grubbs

Boating

In the summertime, Presque Isle becomes a boater's paradise.
Both Lake Erie and Presque Isle Bay offer opportunities for superb sailing,
powerboating, and water sports. For those who don't own a boat, a concession offers
powered and non-powered boats for rent. When the bay freezes over, a few hardy
sailors enjoy iceboating.

Sam Stull

Art Becker

The Marina

Presque Isle Marina is home to nearly 500 boat slips. Additional boat launches are available to the public at various locations throughout the park. As a service, gasoline, diesel fuel, and a sewage pump-out station are all available.

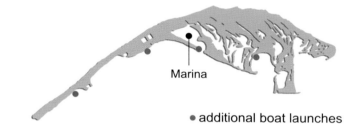

Marina

• additional boat launches

John Buffington

The Channel

The only thing stopping the peninsula from connecting with the mainland along its eastern point, is a shallow channel. The North Pier light sits at the tip of the channel and guards watch over Presque Isle Bay.

Swimming

On hot summer days, the peninsula has provided a perfect place to come and cool down for many generations.

Vitus J. Kaiser

Peninsula Businesses

The Feather

Stull Interpretive Center

Waterworks

Houseboats

Presque Isle Lighthouse

Shelters

Administration Building

Perry Monument

North Pier Light

Coast Guard Station

Structures

Presque Isle Related Businesses

Generating anywhere from 3 to 5 million visitors a year, Presque Isle is the cornerstone of the tourist industry in Erie, Pennsylvania. Not surprisingly, the park has been a magnet for many successful businesses which have set up shop near the park's entrance on Peninsula Drive. Among them are Waldameer Amusement Park, Sara's, Joe Root's Grill, Hansen's Bait Shop, Peninsula Drive-In, the Peninsula Inn, several motels, a campground, and others.

In 1880, a dance hall at the head of Presque Isle was accessible only by ferry.

Historic Presque Isle Businesses

*T*hroughout the years, various entrepreneurs have made use of the peninsula for private business. In the late 1800s, sturgeon were brought onto the peninsula and gutted to sell the eggs as "caviar". Also at this time, Erie Ice Company maintained a storage house on the peninsula and brought daily ice deliveries to Erie. In the 1870s, a resort was in operation which was eventually shut down for its moral impropriety. Additional historic businesses on the peninsula included a sawmill, the Masassauga Hotel, among others.

Perhaps the most creative ideas for businesses on the peninsula came from Joe Root *(see page 48)* - who had visions of starting a hot-air balloon farm - folks could rent a balloon from Joe and be flown to Cleveland or Buffalo. Another idea was to start a feather factory. But probably the most entertaining was Joe's dream of creating a circus. Animals wheeled in wheelbarrows - by other animals - would cross a tightrope from Presque Isle to Erie. Joe would visit the city periodically to get financial investors but surprisingly with no luck.

Political control and lack of successful commercialization of Presque Isle have kept the peninsula relatively safe from private ownership. Thankfully, the combination of establishing Presque Isle as a state park in 1921, and its being named a National Natural Landmark in 1969 have kept Presque Isle accessible to all.

The Feather

The Feather is a work of environmental sculpture by Pittsburgh artist, Angelo Ciotti. The piece which was commissioned by The Erie Art Museum invites the participant to stroll up a thin wooden deck which overlooks a marsh on Presque Isle Bay. As the participant moves up the deck, the ramp widens. This invokes surreal feelings of walking on a giant feather.

After reaching the tip of the overlook, one is greeted with a breathtaking scene across the marsh. About the piece, Ciotti states, "It is a vehicle to the true art...the view".

Angelo Ciotti

Bob Lowry

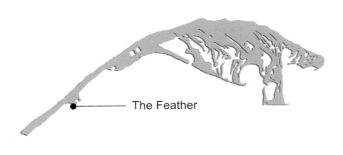
The Feather

Roy Ahlgren

Stull Interpretive Center

The Stull Interpretive Center is located near Barracks Beach on the lakeside of the peninsula. The Center showcases exhibits on the ecological succession of Presque Isle, as well as displays on the park's birds, plants, and wildflowers. Also located in this structure is The Nature Shop at Presque Isle which offers books, t-shirts, artwork and more.

Bob Grubbs

Stull Interpretive Center
and Nature Shop

Waterworks Park

The Waterworks area of the peninsula was developed to act as a clean water source for the City of Erie from 1917 until 1949. Lake Erie water was brought into settling basins and then pumped to the city across Presque Isle Bay. Today, the function of the pumphouse is a zebra mussel control facility for Erie's water supply.

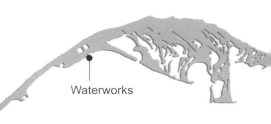

Waterworks

Mary Hamilton

Mark Bowen

John Buffington

Mary Kay Geary

Houseboats

Horseshoe Pond is the current location of a small community of houseboats. The floating homes are owned by a select and lucky few. The houseboat community at Presque Isle began in the 1800s with Russian immigrants, many of whom were professional fishermen. Over the years, the houseboats have moved to various locations at Presque Isle including Misery Bay, Sturgeon Bay, Stinkhole, and along the coastline. By the mid 1960's, legislators attempted to eliminate the houseboats completely. The Houseboat Association fought back, but the owners were given strict guidelines: There must be no more than 24 houseboats, the boats must be painted white, and the dimensions cannot change.

James E. Sabol

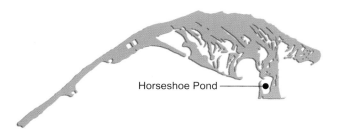

Horseshoe Pond

Presque Isle Lighthouse

By the late 1800s, a booming shipping trade on the Great Lakes resulted in hundreds of lighthouses being built. To prevent Lake Erie mariners from crashing into the peninsula, Presque Isle Lighthouse was constructed in 1872. At that time, there were no roads on the peninsula, so materials were brought across Presque Isle Bay by boat and hauled over to the lake side for construction. During shipping season, April through November, nights were long for the lighthouse keepers. From sunset to sunrise, every 2 to 4 hours the keeper would climb the tower to refuel the oil lamp. While the function of the lighthouse has changed over the years, it is still in use today.

Bruce Kikola

Structural Details of the Lighthouse

- The tower is built of brick, 5 courses thick, which provides strength during Lake Erie storms.
- 57 feet tall, the tower is square on the outside and round on the inside.
- The foundation is built of limestone.
- A winding staircase leading to the light has 78 steps made of iron.
- The residence has 11 rooms.
- The "oil room" or "battery room", at the bottom of the tower was used during the all night vigils.

Mary Hamilton

"Let the lower lights be burning!
Send a gleam across the wave!
Some poor, fainting, struggling seamen
you may rescue you may save."
- Philip R. Bliss 1871

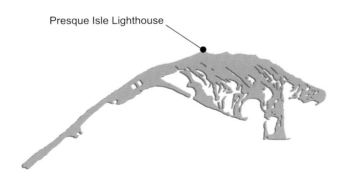

Presque Isle Lighthouse

David Tousey

Kevin-John Jobczynski

James E. Sabol

The original light was a single oil lamp projected through a Fresnel lens. By the 1920s, the light ran on electric power. Today, the light is a 250 watt bulb inside a 300 mm plastic lens. The light is visible 16 miles onto Lake Erie.

Don Dombrowski

11—PRESQUE ISLE LIGHT HOUSE. 1872. ERIE. PA.

courtesy of Edna Huntington

Before a modern road system on the peninsula was built, the lighthouse was very difficult to get to. Charles Waldo, the lighthouse's first keeper called it "the loneliest place on earth."

Lighthouse Keepers

The early keepers were hired by the U.S. Lighthouse Service. In 1939, The Service was incorporated into the U.S. Coast Guard. From 1944-1956 the Lighthouse was vacant. After that period, various families and individuals were recruited to live in the house, although the job of "keeping" the light became significantly easier because of technology. The light is currently maintained by the U.S. Coast Guard while the residence is occupied by a park manager.

Charles Waldo	1873 - 1880
Orrin J McAllister	1880 - 1880 (8 days)
George E. Town	1880 - 1883
Clark M. McCole	1883 - 1886
Lewis Vannatta	1886 - 1891
Louis Walrouse	1891 - 1892
Thomas L. Wilkens	1892 - 1901
Andrew W. Shaw	1901 - 1927 (longest term)
Frank Huntington	1927 - 1944

Adele Larson

Mark Bowen

Joyce Skelly Perowicz

Joyce Skelley Perowicz

Evelyn Askey-Zaleski

Roy Ahlgren

Kevin Irvin

Presque Isle Lighthouse has been the source of inspiration for countless artworks. All too often, while displaying portfolios, regional artists are asked, "But have you done the lighthouse?"

Gary Cardot

Shelters

In the Waterworks area there are three picnic shelters which include electricity, water, and a fireplace. They are available for use with advance reservations.

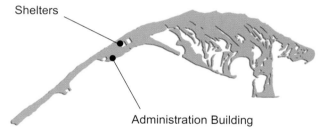

Shelters

Administration Building

Administration Building

Built in 1963, The Administration Building is located two miles past the park's entrance on Peninsula Drive next to Lily Pond.

Art Becker

John Buffington

Perry Monument

Crystal Point, at the peninsula's tip, is home to Perry Monument. The structure, which is a 101 foot obelisk, was built in 1925 to honor Oliver Hazard Perry and the American victory in the Battle of Lake Erie *(see pg 52)*. Perry Monument is built of reinforced concrete faced with royal blue limestone.

Perry Monument

Bob Lowry

North Pier Light

In 1828, a wooden light was built at the tip of the peninsula to stand watch over Presque Isle Bay. The light was eventually crushed by a schooner in 1857, during a Lake Erie storm. The following year a wrought iron light was manufactured in France and shipped to America for assembly at Presque Isle. The location of the light has changed twice, most recently in the 1940s when it was moved to its current location. The Harbor Light is commonly referred to as North Pier Light or Pierhead Light due to its location on North Pier. The light illuminates the channel from Lake Erie into Presque Isle Bay.

Bob Grubbs

John Buffington

U.S. Coast Guard Station

A U.S. Coast Guard station sits at the eastern tip of the peninsula next to the channel between Lake Erie and Presque Isle Bay. This station which has rescued countless mariners in distress over the years, holds the record for one of the largest drug seizures in the history of the Great Lakes.

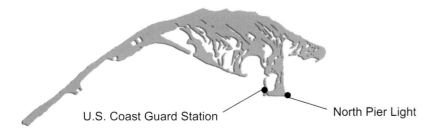

U.S. Coast Guard Station — North Pier Light

Profile of Artists

This book displays artwork from 50 regional artists. The following 7 artists were chosen at random to show how the peninsula is vital to the creative spirit of the region.
• *For a complete list of artists in this book see page 110.*

Vitus J. Kaiser

Vitus Kaiser is a well known and highly respected regional artist. As a landscape painter who primarily works in watercolor, Kaiser frequently chooses Presque Isle as his subject. He views the peninsula as his "outdoor studio".

Presque Isle has become an important piece of land in Vitus Kaiser's career. The painter estimates that he has completed thousands of paintings on the peninsula. Kaiser notes, "Sometimes I will find a spot and just stare for hours without picking up my paintbrush". It is this observation and love of nature that makes his work so outstanding. Kaiser frequently picks compositions from the road less travelled. "I have never been one of those painters who chooses scenes because they sell. If I see a small piece of Queen Ann's Lace gently swaying in the breeze and it catches my eye, then I paint that".

Michael Kaiser

Kaiser's first visit to Presque Isle at 3 months old. (1929)

"My parents would take the family every Sunday, no towels for the kids...when we went swimming we would rub sand on our bodies to dry off."
-V.J. Kaiser

Kevin Irvin

In 1994, Erie artist Kevin Irvin took on an interesting challenge: Visit Presque Isle every single day for an entire year. And so he did. Without fail, day in and day out, 1994 saw Irvin pack up his paint brushes, camera, and writing journal to record his findings on the peninsula.

Throughout his study, Kevin never missed a day. One year later, Irvin hosted a one man art show displaying over 125 works documenting his in-depth and intimate studies of the park. He is still drawn to the peninsula on a regular basis to paint.

"What a wonderful place this is to have at your fingertips, just to come out to think, to look and to listen..."
-Kevin Irvin

Bob Grubbs

Not surprisingly, Presque Isle is a magnet for artists. Erie photographer, Bob Grubbs is no exception.Because Grubbs focuses his photography primarily on nature, the peninsula is overflowing with his kind of subject matter. Being a good nature photographer takes both an educated eye and extreme patience. It is common for Grubbs to prepare many hours, sometimes in harsh weather conditions, for just one shot. Grubbs who finds birds to be his most challenging subject, is also attracted to the peninsula's diverse flora and fauna.

"Presque Isle is a precious site and needs to be protected..."
-Bob Grubbs

Jean Stull

Jean Stull is one of northwestern Pennsylvania's most beloved artists. She is also one of the peninsula's most treasured patrons. The Stull Center, which is the park's nature and wildlife "headquarters", was named for Jean and her late husband, Jim. Stull's love of birds inspired her to co-author **"Birds of Erie County Including Presque Isle"**. She taught art in the Pennsylvania public schools for more than 30 years. As a naturalist, Jean has supported countless regional environmental groups over the years including the Presque Isle State Park Advisory Committee.

E.J. Morris

"My concern now and in the future is that the peninsula may be fragmented and manicured into becoming an image of the places driven through to get there."
-Jean Stull

Reclaiming Beauty

Jim Luhman

A washed up treasure on the shores of Presque Isle is beach glass. Jewelry making sisters, Jennifer Reed and Terri Reed Boyer are known for practicing a little alchemy by incorporating the glass fragments into beautifully designed jewelry. The most common glass colors found on the beach? Brown and green. The rarest colors are red, yellow, and pink.

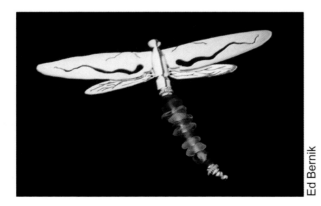

Ed Bernik

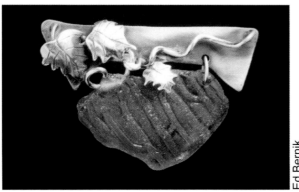

Ed Bernik

Bob Hagle

The assemblages below were made from discarded objects found on the shores of Presque Isle. Modern day "hunter and gatherer", Fran Schanz created the pieces which hang in his downtown Erie gallery.

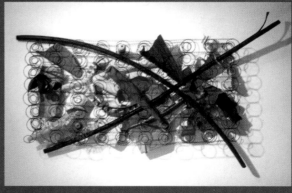

Bob Hagle

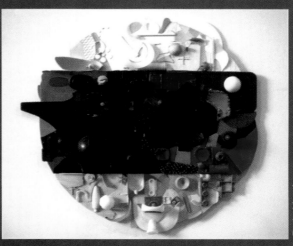

Bob Hagle

Shelle Barron

As noted previously, Presque Isle is a major source of inspiration for regional artists. Your support of local artists enriches the entire community. Many of the artists whose works appear in this book are members of the **Northwestern Pennsylvania Artists Association** and the **Presque Isle Artists Association**.

Historical Sites

Bruce Kikola

① Lighthouse

Built in 1872, the Presque Isle Lighthouse was one of the first lighthouses built on the Great Lakes. (see pg. 84)

② Waterworks

From 1917 to 1949 the City of Erie used this area as a source for clean water. (see pg. 82)

③ Perry Monument

Perry Monument is a 101 foot obelisk built on the tip of Crystal Point. It honors Commodore Oliver Hazard Perry. (see pg. 89)

④ North Pier Light

The North Pier Light stands guard at the southeastern tip of Presque Isle. It lights the channel between Lake Erie and Presque Isle Bay. (see pg. 90)

⑤ Misery Bay

Site where Oliver Hazard Perry and his men spent the winter of 1813. The winter was so harsh that they changed the name from Little Bay to Misery Bay. (see pg. 53)

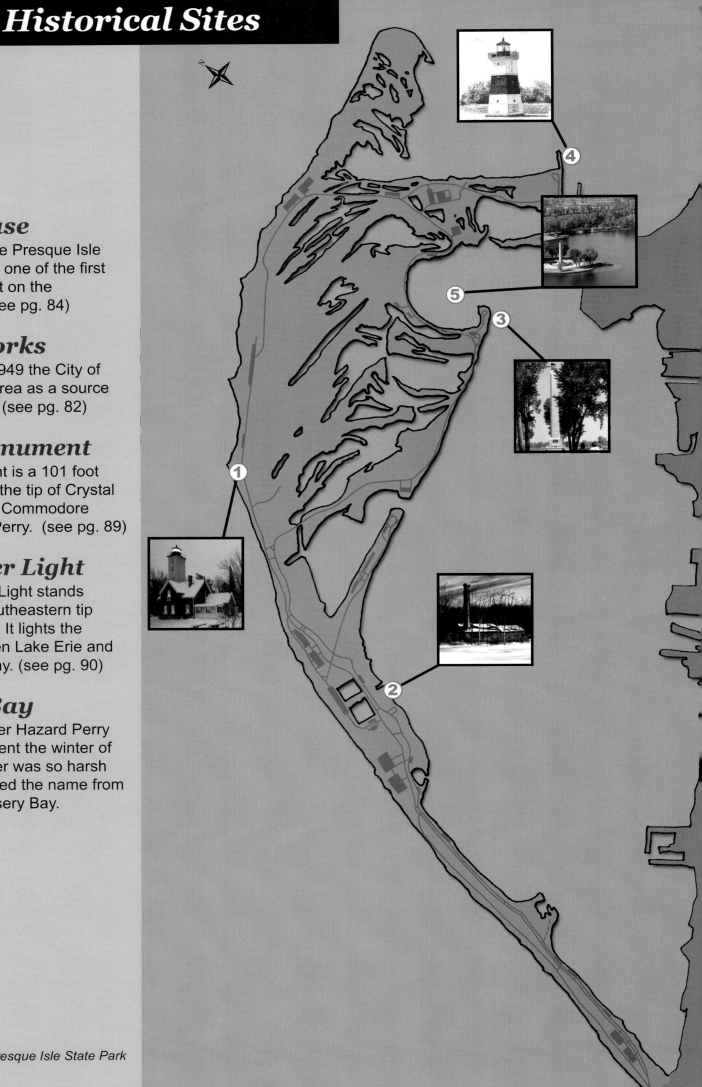

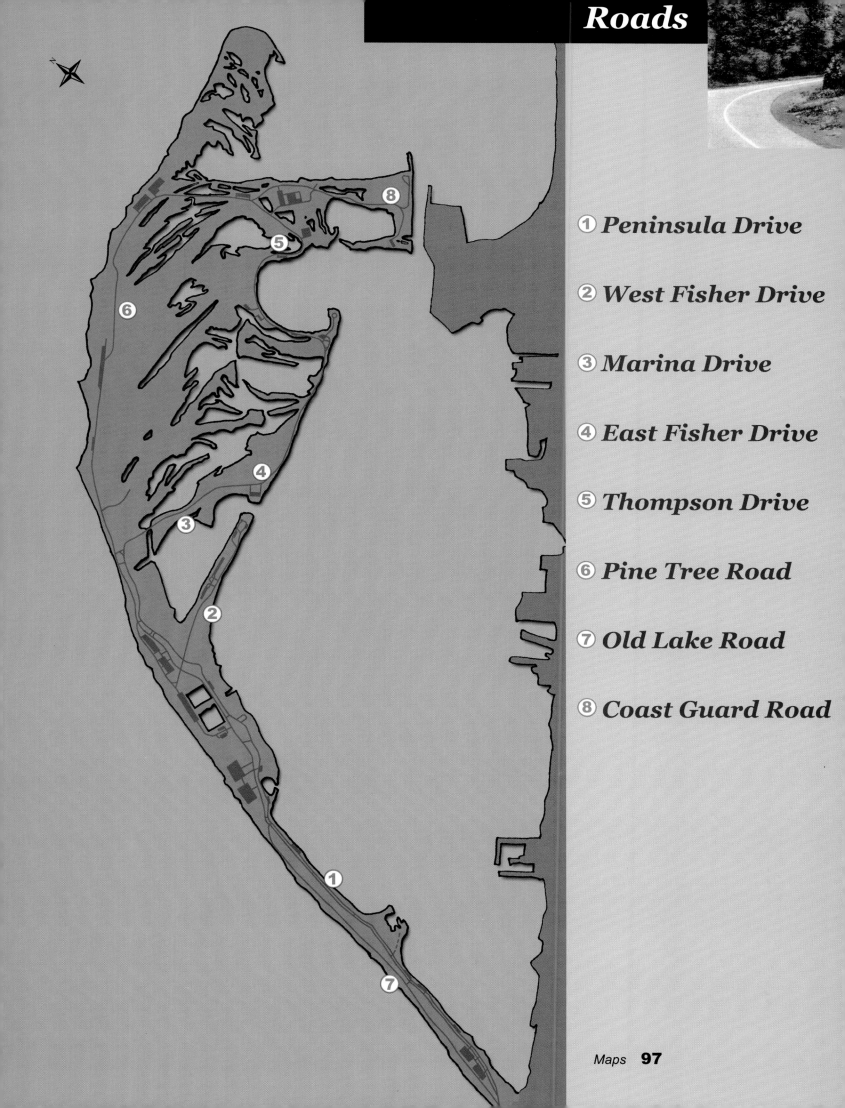

① **Peninsula Drive**

② **West Fisher Drive**

③ **Marina Drive**

④ **East Fisher Drive**

⑤ **Thompson Drive**

⑥ **Pine Tree Road**

⑦ **Old Lake Road**

⑧ **Coast Guard Road**

Beaches

Gary Cardot

(A) *Beach 1 West*
Beach 1
Beach 1 East

(B) *Barracks Beach*
named for former Police Barracks
building (now Stull Center)

(C) *Beach 2*

(D) *Beach 6*
includes sand volleyball
courts and a beach house

(E) *Beach 7 (Waterworks)*
named for Waterworks Park
(see pg. 82)

(F) *Beach 8 (Pettinato Beach)*
named for Presque Isle Lifeguard
legend Frank Pettinato

(G) *Mill Road Beaches*
collection of 6 beaches that incorporates
swimming areas with shaded picnic
facilities

   Stone Jetty
   Duck Pond
   Short Jetty
   Saw Mill
   Ainsworth
   Goddard

(H) *Lighthouse Beach*
location of Presque Isle Lighthouse
(see pg. 84)

(I) *Beach 9 (Pine Tree)*

(J) *Beach 10 (Budny Beach)*
named for Patrick Budny who swam
across Lake Erie from Long Point,
Canada in 1975

(K) *Beach 11*
the most sheltered beach on the
peninsula, also includes playground
equipment and a picnic pavilion

Ponds and Lagoons

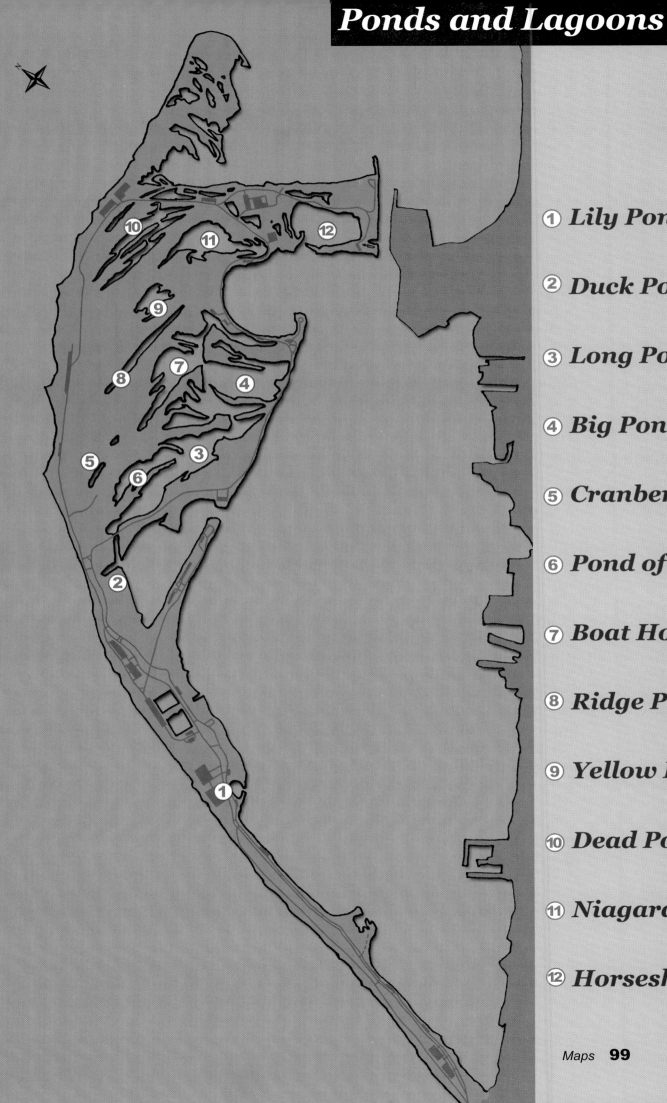

Sam Stull

① *Lily Pond*

② *Duck Pond*

③ *Long Pond*

④ *Big Pond*

⑤ *Cranberry Pond*

⑥ *Pond of the Woods*

⑦ *Boat House Pond*

⑧ *Ridge Pond*

⑨ *Yellow Bass Pond*

⑩ *Dead Pond*

⑪ *Niagara Pond*

⑫ *Horseshoe Pond*

John Horstman

1 *Self-guiding Interpretive Trail*
begins at the Stull Interpretive Center and
hike from the beach to the forest (.5 miles)

2 *Fox Trail*
winds through wooded swamps and
Oak-Maple forests (.5 miles)

3 *Old Gas Well Trail*
passes a gas well that produces gas used
at Presque Isle (.5 miles)

4 *Canoe Portage Trail*
short walk between sand dunes and
forest which connects Pettinato Beach
to Marina Lake (.25 miles)

5 *Ridge Trail*
follows the edge of Cranberry Pond
(.5 miles)

6 *Marsh Trail*
bisects Cranberry Pond (.25 miles)

7 *Sidewalk Trail*
originally constructed by the U.S. Lighthouse
Service as a path from the Presque Isle
Lighthouse to the U.S. Lighthouse Service
boathouse in Misery Bay (1.25 miles)

8 *Dead Pond Trail*
leads through several distinct ecological
zones (2 miles)

9 *A-Trail*
connects Pine Tree Picnic Area to
Dead Pond Trail (.2 miles)

10 *B-Trail*
connects Pine Tree Road to
Dead Pond Trail (.25 miles)

11 *Pine Tree Trail*
located along this trail are the remains of the
Biology Field Lab that was used to study
plant succesion on Presque Isle (.7 miles)

12 *Gull Point Trail*
begins at the kiosk east of beach 10
and loops through Gull Point
also leads to an observation
platform for viewing shorebirds (1.5 miles)

13 *North Pier Trail*
follows the shoreline between North Pier
and Beach 11. An old WWII firing range
may be seen along this trail (.7 miles)

14 *Graveyard Pond Trail*
follows the shore along Graveyard Pond,
which was the final resting place for many
of Perry's men (.75 miles)

15 *Long Pond Trail*
follows the shoreline along Long Pond,
located along the way is a popular fishing
spot and a scenic view of the lagoon (1 mile)

16 *Duck Pond Trail*
trail begins at Duck Pond and intersects
the Canoe Portage trail and connects with
the Old Gas Well Trail. (.5 miles)

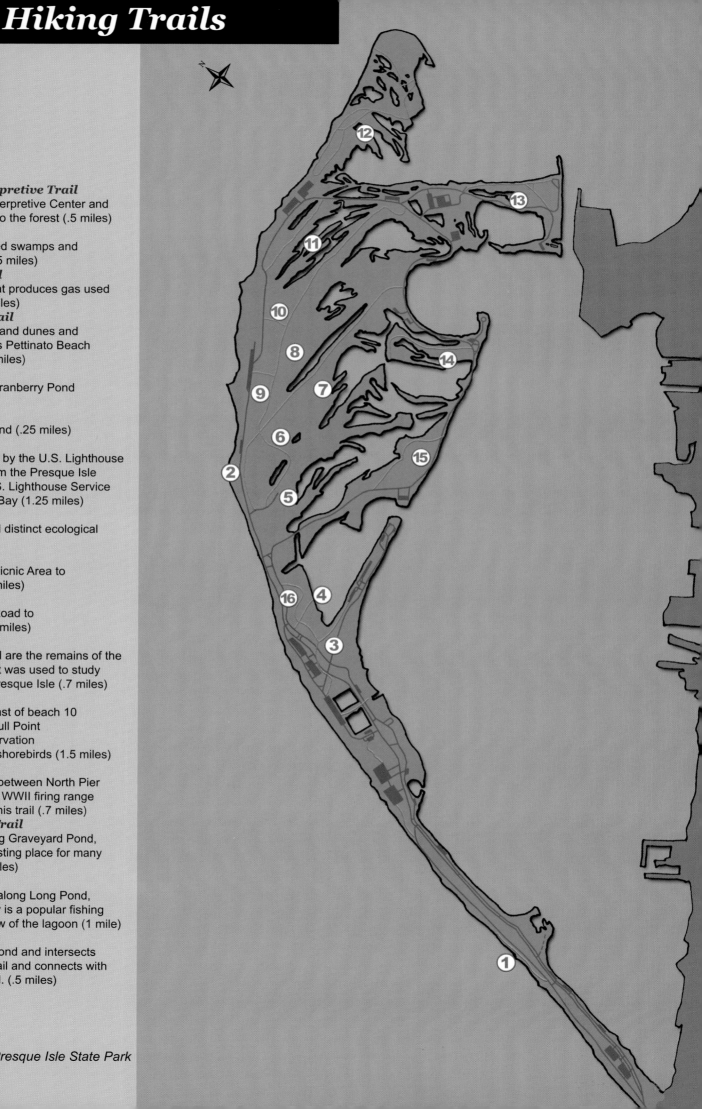

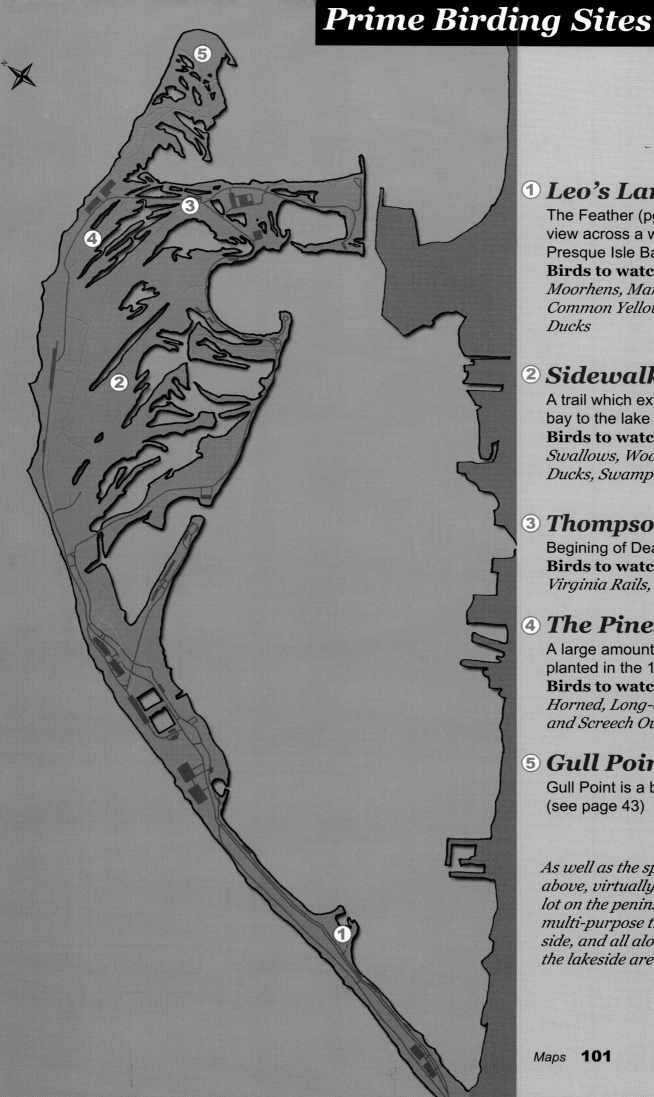

Prime Birding Sites

Sam Stull

① Leo's Landing

The Feather (pg. 80) offers a view across a wetland into Presque Isle Bay.

Birds to watch for: *Common Moorhens, Marsh Wrens, and Common Yellowthroats, Wood Ducks*

② Sidewalk Trail

A trail which extends from the bay to the lake side.

Birds to watch for: *Tree Swallows, Woodpeckers, Wood Ducks, Swamp Sparrows, herons*

③ Thompson Circle

Begining of Dead Pond Trail.

Birds to watch for: *Soras, Virginia Rails, and bitterns.*

④ The Pines

A large amount of pine trees planted in the 1930's.

Birds to watch for: *Great Horned, Long-eared, Saw-whet, and Screech Owls.*

⑤ Gull Point

Gull Point is a bird sanctuary. (see page 43)

As well as the spots mentioned above, virtually any parking lot on the peninsula, the multi-purpose trail on the bay side, and all along the beach on the lakeside are great for birding.

Jean Stull

Bruce Kikola

View of Erie, Pennsylvania from Presque Isle

Joseph Plavcan
from the collection of The Erie Art Museum

A group of Civil War reenactors enjoy a quick break to rollerblade around Crystal Point.

Bibliography and Suggested Reading

Birds of Erie County Pennsylvania Including Presque Isle

Jean Stull, James A. Stull, Gerald M. McWilliams. Allegheny Press

James E. Sabol

James E. Sabol. Morgenstern & Reilly, Inc.

Lightkeeper's Legacy: A Personal History of Presque Isle

Loretta A. Brandon. Erie County Historical Society Publications

Lost Erie: The Vanished Heritage of City and County

John R. Claridge. Erie County Historical Society Publications

Presque Isle: A Place for All Seasons

E.V. and Gayle Giza

Home Port Erie: Voices of Silent Images

Robert J. McDonald and David Frew. Erie County Historical Society Publications

The Birds of Pennsylvania

Gerald M. McWilliams and Daniel W. Brauning. Cornell University Press

Presque Isle

Partnership

The mission statement of the Presque Isle Partnership is very direct:

"to preserve, protect, and enhance Presque Isle"

Fulfilling this mission is not easy... it demands that the Partnership convince park users to quit taking the Park for granted... to realize that the peninsula is our "backyard"... that it belongs to us...not the state.

Founded in 1994, The Presque Isle Partnership accepted the challenge of that mission statement and developed a fund raising strategy to raise the needed funds for park improvements, control of invasive plants, and a field research station to explore many of the environmental unknowns at Presque Isle.

The continuing success of the Partnership has been impressive...with a strong blend of community and corporate support for ongoing changes at Presque Isle. Obviously, more can be done... and obviously more people need to be convinced that this "crown jewel" of the state park system can only be made complete by those who love it.

Since 1994 nearly a million dollars has been raised by the Partnership... proof that the concept of "partnering" can be effective... and proof that more can...and will...be done in the future.

- Don Guerrein
Founder

Erie County Historical Society and Museum

Presque Isle State Park Contact Information

Presque Isle State Park
814-833-7424
PO Box 8510   Erie, Pa 16505

Stull Interpretive Center
814-833-0351

Marina Office
(seasonal) 814-833-0176

Lifeguard Headquarters
(seasonal) 814-833-0526

State Parks and Forests 1-888-PA PARKS
PA Bureau of State Parks
P.O. Box 8551 Harrisburg, PA 17105-8551

National Park Service 215-597-7018
Office of Public Inquiries (Rm. 1013)
Department of the Interior
1849 C Street, Northwest
Washington, DC 20240

Erie Area Convention and Visitors Bureau and Erie Area Chamber of Commerce (814) 454-7191
1006 State Street Erie, Pa. 16501

Fishing /Boating 1-717-657-4518

Wildlife/Hunting/State Game Lands 1-717-787-4250

Erie Maritime Museum (814) 452-2744
150 East Front St. Erie, Pa 16507

WEB PAGES OF INTEREST

Pennsylvania www.state.pa.us

State Parks www.dcnr.state.pa.us

National Parks www.nps.gov

Erie www.eriepa.com

Fishing www.fish.state.pa.us

Wildlife/Hunting www.pge.state.pa.us

Flagship Niagara www.brigniagara.org

Joyce Skelley Perowicz

The Artists

Thank you for sharing your gift
and capturing the beauty that is Presque Isle

Evelyn Anderson, Roy Ahlgren, Shelle Barron, Susan Hosford Beck,

Art Becker, Laura Beichner O.S.B., Mark Bowen, Terri Reed Boyer, John Buffington, Dan Byler,

Mike Campbell, Gary Cardot, Angelo Ciotti, Louis A. Colussi, John Silk Deckard, Don Dombrowski,

Judy Emling, John Fontecchio, Mary Kay Geary, Bob Grubbs, Bob Hagle, Mary Hamilton, John Horstman, Kevin Irvin,

Kevin John Jobczynski, Jostens Photography Studio, Michael Kaiser, Vitus J. Kaiser, Denise Keim, Bruce Kikola,

Eric LaPrice, Adele Larsen, Bob Lowry, Jim McEnery, Ann Muczynski O.S.B., Anthony Orlando, Jack Paluh,

Joyce Skelley Perowicz, Margret Ann Pilewski O.S.B., Joseph Plavcan, Jennifer Reed, James E. Sabol,

Fran Schanz, Lee Steadman, Vi Bebell Steinbacher, Jean Stull, Sam Stull, Wilda Sundberg,

Lucia Surmik O.S.B., Dave Tousey, Jeff Urraro, Charles Ventrello,

Kate Weber, Lynn Weissert O.S.B., Evelyn Askey-Zaleski,

This book was made possible through the generosity and support from the following...

Kristen Alaimo, Annita Andrick, Bob Allshouse, Evelyn Anderson, Sherrie Arndt, Sarah Barrows, Vicki Bowman, Gerald Beck, Department of Conservation and Natural Resources, Don Bernardo, Dan Berke, Joby Clark, Crowner/King Architects, Gretchen Gallo, Mike Campbell, Nicole Canter, John Claridge, Dave Chrzanowski, Toby Cunningham, Matta D, Anne DeSarro, Erie County Historical Society and Museum, Digital Alchemy, Marg Estes, David Frew, Larry Gauriloff, Don and Paula Guerrein, Ivan Held, Nan Held, John Herr, Jody Stanniunis Hopper, Edna Huntington, John Hyatt, Dev Jana, Candy Jaruszewicz, Amy Lynn Kosmack, Eric LaPrice, Ned Lehrian, John Leemhuis, Harry Leslie, Arthur Levin, Janice Locke, Joanne Lyons, Stacey Manz, Char Markowitz, Rebecca Martin, Edwin Masteller, Gerald McWilliams, Diane Clark Moran, Don Muller, Joe Mehl, Randy Neyer, Aimee Nicolia, One World Tribe, Anthony Orlando, Janet Orr, Chad Penn, Dave Richards, Governor Tom Ridge, Karen Ruda, Mayor Joyce Savocchio, Loretta Schaal, Janet Schulz, Rod Shaffer, Derf Sieber, Anita Smith, Jacki Speigel, Norm and Marie Stark, Jean Stull, Carl Sundberg, Cynthia Taylor, Beth Theobald, John Vanco, Elly Vahey, Rob Veres, Bob Walker, Gloria Walker, Sally Walker, Erik Walker, Stan Zagorski

*with special thanks
to all of the artists
listed on the previous page*

Art Becker